Highlights of the 40's & 50's

40's

1941
1942
1943 1944 1945
& 1948 1946 1947
1949

50's

Exclusive Selling Agent:
Creative Concepts Publishing Corporation
410 Bryant Circle, Box 848
Ojai, California 93024

Catalog No. 07-1092 • ISBN No. 1-56922-004-2

CONTENTS

SOUVENIR PHOTO SECTION 4
ALL I HAVE TO DO IS DREAM
Made Popular by The Everly Brothers 12
ARE YOU SINCERE?
Made Popular by Andy Williams 15
BE MY LIFE'S COMPANION
Made Popular by The Mills Brothers 18
BORN TOO LATE
Made Popular by The Poni-Tails 22
BROKEN-HEARTED MELODY
Made Popular by Sarah Vaughan 24
CANDY
Made Popular by Jo Stafford, Johnny Mercer & The Pied Pipers 26
CARA MIA
Made Popular by David Whitfield 28
CATCH A FALLING STAR
Made Popular by Perry Como 30
COLONEL BOGEY MARCH
Made Popular from the Motion Picture "The Bridge On The River Kwai" 43
DO YOU KNOW WHAT IT MEANS TO MISS NEW ORLEANS?
Made Popular by Billie Holiday with Louis Armstrong 32
DON'T SIT UNDER THE APPLE TREE
Made Popular by The Andrew Sisters 36
DON'T TAKE YOUR LOVE FROM ME
Made Popular by Mildred Bailey 40
DON'T YOU KNOW?
Made Popular by Della Reese 46
DUNGAREE DOLL
Made Popular by Eddie Fisher 48
(The) END
Made Popular by Earl Grant 54
ENDLESSLY
Made Popular by Brook Benton 51
GRADUATION DAY
Made Popular by The Four Freshman 56
HARLEM NOCTURNE
Made Popular by Ray Noble & His Orchestra 58
HAVE YOU HEARD?
Made Popular by Joni James 66
HEART
Made Popular by Eddie Fisher 68
HEY THERE
Made Popular by Rosemary Clooney 70
HIGH NOON
Made Popular by Frankie Lane 72
HOLIDAY FOR STRINGS
Made Popular by David Rose & His Orchestra 61
(The) HUCKLEBUCK
Made Popular by Tommy Dorsey & His Orchestra 76
I GOT IT BAD (And That Ain't Good)
Made Popular by Duke Ellington & His Orchestra 78
I'LL WALK ALONE
Made Popular by Dinah Shore 82
IN THE WEE SMALL HOURS OF THE MORNING
Made Popular by Frank Sinatra 88
INTERMEZZO (A Love Story)
Made Popular by Guy Lombardo & His Orchestra 90
IT STARTED ALL OVER AGAIN
Made Popular by Tommy Dorsey & His Orchestra with Frank Sinatra 85
IT'S BEEN A LONG, LONG TIME
Made Popular by Harry James & His Orchestra with Kitty Kallen 94
IT'S JUST A MATTER OF TIME
Made Popular by Brook Benton 97
I'VE HEARD THAT SONG BEFORE
Made Popular by Harry James & His Orchestra with Helen Forrest 100
JAVA JIVE
Made Popular by The Ink Spots 103

CONTENTS

JERSEY BOUNCE
Made Popular by Benny Goodman & His Orchestra 106

LOVE IS ALL WE NEED
Made Popular by Tommy Edwards 108

MAIRZY DOATS
Made Popular by The Merry Macs 110

MAY YOU ALWAYS
Made Popular by The McGuire Sisters 112

MIDNIGHT SUN
Made Popular by Ella Fitzgerald 114

MISIRLOU
Made Popular by Jan August 116

MY FOOLISH HEART
Made Popular by Billy Eckstine 120

NATURE BOY
Made Popular by Nat King Cole 122

NIGHT TRAIN
Made Popular by Jimmy Forrest 128

NINA NEVER KNEW
Made Popular by Joe Mooney 130

(The) OLD LAMPLIGHTER
Made Popular by Sammy Kay & His Orchestra with Billy Williams 125

ORANGE COLORED SKY
Made Popular by Nat King Cole 132

PAPER DOLL
Made Popular by The Mills Brothers 134

PEG O' MY HEART
Made Popular by The Harmonicats 137

PLEASE MR. SUN
Made Popular by Johnny Ray 140

PRETEND
Made Popular by Nat King Cole 142

QUE SERA, SERA (Whatever Will Be, Will Be)
Made Popular by Doris Day 144

RAGS TO RICHES
Made Popular by Tony Bennett 146

(Get Your Kicks On) ROUTE 66
Made Popular by Nat King Cole 148

SEE YOU IN SEPTEMBER
Made Popular by The Tempos 154

SHOO FLY PIE AND APPLE PAN DOWDY
Made Popular by Dinah Shore 151

SINCERELY
Made Popular by The McGuire Sisters 156

SOMEWHERE ALONG THE WAY
Made Popular by Nat King Cole 159

TAMMY
Made Popular by Debbie Reynolds 162

THIS COULD BE THE START OF SOMETHING BIG
Made Popular by Steve Lawrence & Eydie Gorme 164

'TIS AUTUMN
Made Popular by Les Brown & His Orchestra with Ralph Young 168

(The) TWELFTH OF NEVER
Made Popular by Johnny Mathis 171

TWO DIFFERENT WORLDS
Made Popular by Don Rondo 174

WAKE THE TOWN AND TELL THE PEOPLE
Made Popular by Les Brown & His Orchestra and Chorus 176

WE'LL BE TOGETHER AGAIN
Made Popular by Frankie Lane 182

WHEN THE SWALLOWS COME BACK TO CAPISTRANO
Made Popular by The Ink Spots 179

WHO WOULDN'T LOVE YOU?
Made Popular by Kay Kyser & His Orchestra 184

WHY DON'T YOU BELIEVE ME
Made Popular by Joni James 190

WONDERFUL! WONDERFUL!
Made Popular by Johnny Mathis 187

LOUIS ARMSTRONG

JOHNNY DESMOND

BING CROSBY AND FRANK SINATRA

BILLIE HOLIDAY

IRVING BERLIN AND DINAH SHORE

HARRY JAMES

All I Have To Do Is Dream

Words and Music by Boudleaux Bryant

© 1958 and renewed 1986 HOUSE OF BRYANT PUBLICATIONS
All Rights Reserved

Are You Sincere?

Words and Music by Wayne P. Walker

© 1957 and renewed 1985 WAYNE WALKER MUSIC, INC. and CEDARWOOD PUBLISHING CO., INC.
All Rights Reserved

Be My Life's Companion

Words and Music by Milton DeLugg and Bob Hillard

© 1951 and renewed 1979 AMY DEE MUSIC CORP.
All Rights Reserved

Candy

Words and Music by Mack David, Joan Whitney and Alex Kramer

Moderately slow

©1944 and renewed 1972 KRAMER-WHITNEY, INC. and HARRY VON TILZER MUSIC PUBLISHING CO.
All Rights Reserved

Catching A Falling Star

Words and Music by Lee Pockriss and Paul Vance

© 1957 and renewed 1985 MUSIC SALES CORPORATION and EMILY MUSIC CORP.
All Rights Reserved

Do You Know What It Means To Miss New Orleans?

Lyric by Eddie DeLange
Music by Louis Alter

© 1946 and renewed 1974 LOUIS ALTER MUSIC and SCARSDALE MUSIC CORP.
All Rights Reserved

Don't Sit Under The Apple Tree

Words and Music by Charles Tobias, Lew Brown and Sam Stept

© 1942 and renewed 1970 CHED MUSIC and SBK/ROBBINS MUSIC
All Rights Reserved

Chorus, *Brightly*
F C7 F D7-9
Don't Sit Un-der The Ap-ple Tree with an-y-one else but me,
mp
Gm7 C7 Gm7 C7 F Gm7 C7 F C7 Gm7 C7
An-y-one else but me, An-y-one else but me, No! No! No!
F C7 F Cm6 D7
Just re-mem-ber that I've been true to no-bod-y else but you, So
G7 Gm7 C7 F Bb F Gm7
just be true to me,

Don't go walk-ing down lov-ers' lane with an-y-one else but me, An-y-one else but me, An-y-one else but me, No! No! No! Don't start show-ing off all your charms in some-bod-y else's arms, You must be true to me. I'm so a-fraid that the plans we made un-der-neath those moon-lit skies Will fade a-way and you're

bound to stray if the stars get in your eyes, So, Don't Sit Un-der The

Ap-ple Tree with an-y-one else but me, You're my L -

1. O - V - E. 2. E.

Don't Take Your Love From Me

Words and Music by Henry Nemo

Moderately

You could take my cas-tle, that's if I had a cas-tle, and I'd
You could take my trea-sure, that's if I had a trea-sure, and I'd

1. miss it for just a while,
2. face pov-er-ty with a smile,

But there's one thing I ask of you, one thing you must nev-er do. Tear a

© 1941 and renewed 1969 INDANO MUSIC CO.
All Rights Reserved

Refrain:

star from out the sky_____ and the sky feels blue,_____ Tear a
take the wings from birds_____ so that they can't fly,_____ Would you

pet - al from a rose_____ and the rose weeps too._____
take the o - cean's roar_____ and leave

Take your heart a - way from mine and mine will sure - ly break, My life is yours to make, so please keep the spark a-wake. Would you just a sigh? All this your heart won't let you do, This is what I beg of you, Don't Take Your Love From Me.

From the Motion Picture "The Bridge On The River Kwai"
Colonel Bogey March
Words and Music by Kenneth J. Alford (F.J. Ricketts)

Arr. by Bill Irwin

© 1992 PORTSIDE MUSIC (ASCAP)
All Rights Reserved

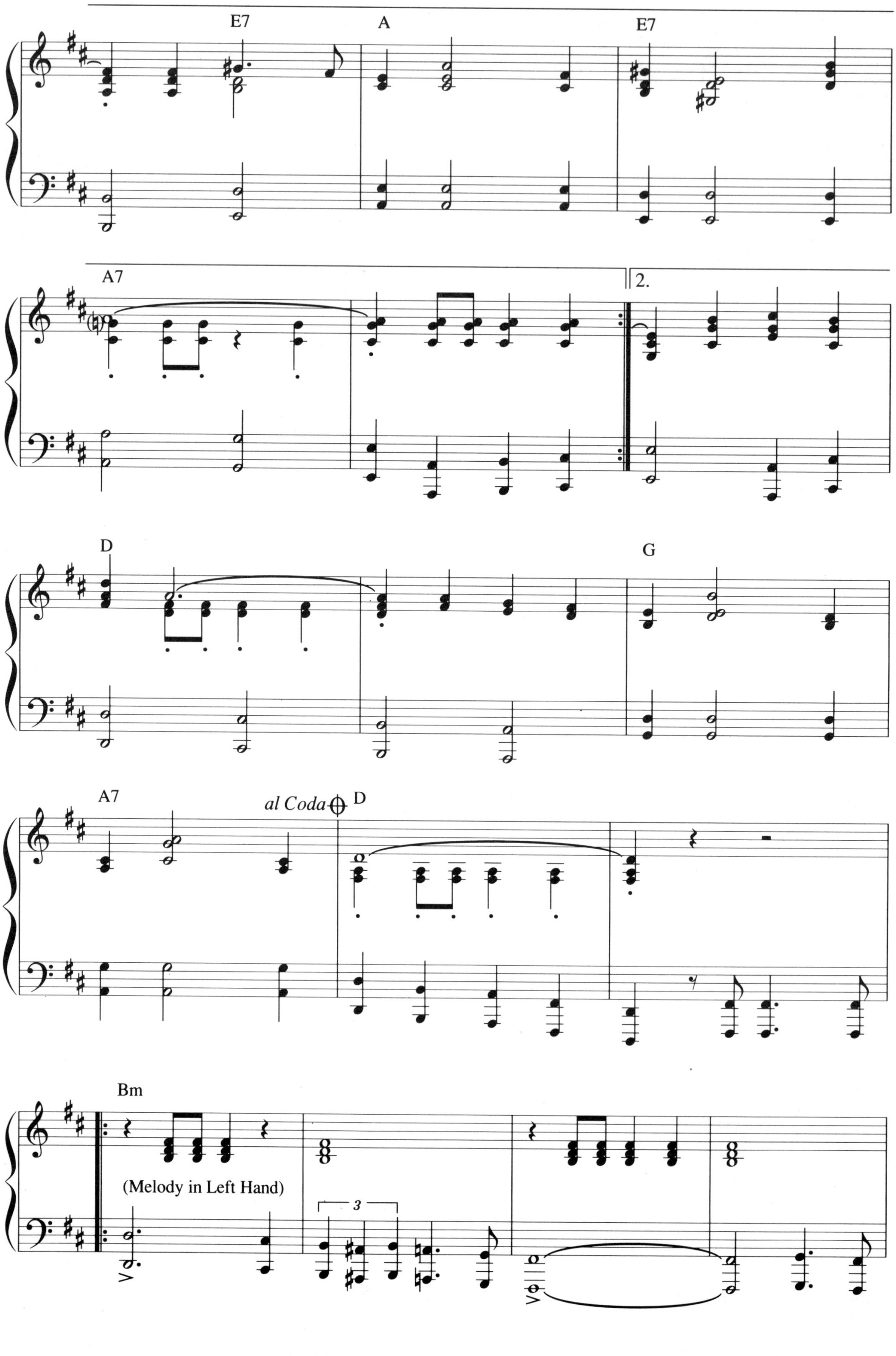
E7
A
E7
A7
2.
D
G
A7
al Coda
D
Bm
(Melody in Left Hand)
3

45

Don't You Know?

Words and Music by Bobby Worth

Slowly, with great expression

DON'T YOU KNOW? _____ I have fall-en in love with you, _____ For the rest of my whole life through. _____ DON'T YOU KNOW? _____ I was yours from the

© 1958 and renewed 1986 ALEXIS MUSIC, INC.
All Rights Reserved

ver-y day ___ That you hap-pened to come my way. ___ Can't you see ___ I'm un-der your spell? ___ By the look in my eyes, ___ Can't you tell, Can't you tell? DON'T YOU KNOW? ___ Ev-'ry beat of my heart keeps cry-ing out, "I want you so!" ___ DON'T YOU KNOW? KNOW? ___

Dungaree Doll

Words by Ben Raleigh
Music by Sherman Edwards

With a solid beat

(Boy:) DUN-GA-REE DOLL! DUN-GA-REE DOLL! Paint your in-i-tials
(Girl:) I'm your DUN-GA-REE DOLL! DUN-GA-REE DOLL! I'll paint my in-i-tials

on my jeans, So ev-'ry-one in town will know we go a-roun' To
on your jeans, So ev-'ry-one in town will know we go a-roun' To

geth-er, to-geth-er, to-geth-er._____ DUN-GA-REE DOLL!
geth-er, to-geth-er, to-geth-er._____ I'm your DUN-GA-REE DOLL!

© 1955 and renewed 1983 KEITH-VALERIE MUSIC CORP., a division of Music Sales Corporation (ASCAP)
All Rights Reserved

DUN-GA-REE DOLL! Paste my picture on your sleeve, So ev-'ry-one can see that you be-long to me, For-ev-er, for-ev-er, for-ev-er. I want you to wear my or-ange sweat-er, The beat-up sweat-er with the high school let-ter. Gon-na make a chain of

DUN-GA-REE DOLL! I'll paste your picture on my sleeve, So ev-'ry-one can see that you be-long to me, For-ev-er, for-ev-er, for-ev-er. I wan-na wear your or-ange sweat-er, The beat-up sweat-er with the high school let-ter. Gon-na make a chain of

Cm6
A7
D7
(tacet)
pa - per clips_ And chain us to - geth - er, while I kiss your lips. You
pa - per clips_ And chain us to - geth - er, while you kiss my lips. I'm your
G
B7
E7
DUN-GA-REE DOLL! DUN-GA-REE DOLL! Prom-ise me you nev-er will fall for
DUN-GA-REE DOLL! DUN-GA-REE DOLL! Prom-ise you I nev-er will fall for
A9
Am7
G
Em7
an - y oth - er guy, Tell me you are my DUN - GA - REE, DUN-GA - REE,
an - y oth - er guy, Don't you know that I'm your DUN - GA - REE, DUN-GA - REE,
Am7
G
A7
D7
1. G
A9
D7
2. G
DUN-GA-REE, DUN-GA-REE, DUN-GA - REE, DUN-GA-REE DOLL! DOLL!
DUN-GA-REE, DUN-GA-REE, DUN-GA - REE, DUN-GA-REE DOLL! I'm your DOLL!
sf

Endlessly

Words and Music by Clyde Otis and Brook Benton

Brightly

f Very sustained

High-er than the high-est moun-tain _____ and deep-er than the deep-est sea, _____ That's how I will love _____ you dar-ling _____ END-LESS-LY _____

© 1957 and renewed 1985 IZA MUSIC CORP.
All Rights Reserved

Soft-er than the gen-tle breez-es and stron-ger than a wild oak tree. That's how I will hold you dar-ling ENDLESSLY. Oh, my love you are my heav-en You are my king-dom you are my crown.

Bb Am Dm G7
Oh, my love you're all I prayed for you were made for
C7 F Bb
these arms to sur - round. Faith-ful as a morn - ing
F Bb F
sun - rise and sa-cred as a love can be,
Bb Bdim F Dm
That's how I will love you
F Bb F F
darling ENDLESS-LY. LY. ENDLESS
1. 2.
Repeat and fade out

The End (Of A Rainbow)

Lyric by Sid Jacobson
Music by Jimmy Krondes

Moderato, with feeling

At THE END of a rain-bow, You'll find a pot of gold, At THE END of a sto-ry, You'll find it's all been told; But our love has a treas-ure Our hearts can al-ways spend, And it has a sto-ry with-out an-y end. At THE END of a riv-er, The wa-ter stops its

© 1958 and renewed 1986 J.K. Music
All Rights Reserved

G7 (opt.) C Em Dm7 G7
flow, At THE END of a high-way, There's no place you can go; But just
C Am7 1. Dm7 G7 C G♯dim Am
tell me you love me And you are on-ly mine, And our love will go
Am7 Dm7 G7 C (opt.) 2. Dm7 G7 Dm7 G7
on Till THE END of time. At THE you are on-ly mine, And our
8va
mf
C Am Dm G9 G7 C
love will go on Till THE END of time.
Am7 Dm7 G7 C
Till THE END of time.
rall.

Graduation Day

Words by Noel Sherman
Music by Joe Sherman

Moderately

It's a time for joy, a time for tears, a time we'll treas-ure thru the years

We'll re-mem-ber al-ways GRAD-U-A-TION DAY. At the

Sen-ior Prom we danced till three, and then you gave your heart to me

© 1956 and renewed 1984 ERASMUS MUSIC
All Rights Reserved

Dm7 G7 C A7-9 Dm7 G9 C
We'll re-mem-ber al-ways GRAD-U-A-TION DAY.
Gm7 C7 Fmaj7 F F#dim Gm7 C7 Fmaj7 F6
Tho' we leave in sor-row all the joys we've known,
Am7 D7 Gmaj7 G G#dim Am7 D7 Dm7 G7
We can face to-mor-row know-ing we'll nev-er walk a-lone. When the
C Dm7 C F C Dm7 C Ebdim
I-vy Walls are far be-hind, no mat-ter where our path may wind,
Dm7 G7 C A7-9 Dm7 G9
we'll re-mem-ber al-ways GRAD-U-A-TION DAY!
1. C Ab7 G7
It's a
2. C F9 Cmaj7
DAY!
rit.

Harlem Nocturne

Words by Dick Rogers
Music by Earle Hagen

© MCMXL, MCMLXVI, MCMLI SHAPIRO, BERNSTEIN & CO., INC.
All Rights Reserved

E♭ E♭7 D7 Gm6 C9 Gm6
For-ev-er is haun-ting me.
G♭9 F9 B♭7 Fm7 B♭7 Fm7 B♭7 Fm7
The mel-o-dy clings A-round my heart strings It won't let me go when I'm
B♭7 B7 B♭7 E♭7 B♭m7 E♭7 B♭m7
lone-ly I hear it in dreams And some-how it seems It
(Tacit)
F7 B♭7 Fm7
makes me weep and I can't sleep An in-di-go tune It
B♭7 Fm7 B♭7 Fm7 B♭7 B7 B♭7
sings to the moon The lone-some re-frain of a lo-ver The

mel-o-dy sighs___ It laughs and it cries ___ A moan in blue that wails the long night thru.___ Tho' with the dawn it's gone__ The mel-o-dy lives e - ver _____ For lone-ly hearts to learn _____ Of love in a Har-lem Noc-turne.__

Holiday For Strings

Words by Sammy Gallop
Music by David Rose

Brightly

When I see you smile at me, I hear a haunt-ing mel-o-dy and
I sur-ren-der to the ten-der thrill it brings a
HOL-I-DAY FOR STRINGS, sweet mu-sic all a-round me,

© 1943, 1944 and renewed 1971, 1972 SAMMY GALLOP MUSIC and WB MUSIC CORP.
All Rights Reserved

Soft-ly as the song be-gins, I hear a host of vi-o-lins, or can it on-ly be my lone-ly heart that sings a HOL-I-DAY FOR STRINGS, be-cause your love has found me

Broadly

Thru the night, _____ A love song fills the air, _____ I hear it ev-'ry-where, _____ so sweet-ly tell-ing me I'm yours com - plete - ly; Breez - es sigh, _____ a new born rhap - so - dy _____ When you are close to me, _____ there's mu - sic, Nev - er heard such love - ly mu - sic.

When you're gone it fades a-way, but when we meet I hear it play, As from a-bove, a song of love comes sweet and clear, When-ev-er you are near, the an-gels play a HOL-I-DAY FOR

Have You Heard?

Words and Music by Lew Douglas, Frank Lavere, and Roy Rodde

Moderately slow

HAVE YOU HEARD? Who's kiss-ing {him/her} now Do you think {he's/she's} blue Did {he/she} say we're thru Has {he/she} found some-one new Have you seen The way {he/she} looks now Does {he/she} act the same when {he/she} hears my name Does {he/she} say who's to

© 1952 and renewed 1980 BRANDON MUSIC CO.
All Rights Reserved

C E G#7 A Edim
blame My arms are emp - ty, my nights are long and lone - ly, I
A E G B7 C
miss {him {her so Eacn new to - mor - row, can on - ly bring me
C7 B7+ B7 G9 G7 C B7+ Em
sor - row, I love {him {her so HAVE YOU HEARD?
F 3 C Dm7 G7 Gm A7
Of their wed-ding day Ru-mors come and go still I'd like to know
Fm G7 C Gm A7 Dm7 G7b9 1. C Cdim Dm7 G7b9 2. C
if it's true, won't you tell me HAVE YOU HEARD? HEARD?
rit.

From *"Damn Yankees"*

Heart

Words and Music by Richard Adler and Jerry Ross

Moderato

Gm7 C11 Gm7-5 F Cm7 F F7+5
Tacet
Wait-'ll next year and hope. when your luck is bat-tin' ze-ro, Get your chin up off the
Bbmaj7 Bb6 Dm7 G7 C7 Cdim
Tacet
floor; Mis-ter, you can be a he-ro, You can o-pen an-y door, there's noth-in' to it, but to
C7 D7+5 Gm7 Db9 C7 C7+5 Fmaj7
do it, You've Got-ta Have Heart, Miles 'n' miles 'n' miles of heart,
F6 D7 Dm7 G7 Gm7 C11 Cm6 D7
Oh, it's fine to be a gen-ius of course, but keep that old horse be-fore the cart,
Gm7 C7 F F#dim Gm7 D7+5 F Bb9 Bdim F6
First You've Got-ta Have Heart! You've Got-ta Have Heart.
8va

Hey There

Words and Music by Richard Adler and Jerry Ross

Slowly and expressively

Hey There, ___ you with the stars in your eyes, ___ Love nev-er made a fool of you, You used to be too wise! ___ Hey There, ___ you on that high fly-ing cloud, Tho' she won't throw a crumb to you, You think some-day she'll come to you; ___ Bet-ter for-get her, ___

© 1954 and renewed 1982 RICHARD ADLER MUSIC and J.J. ROSS CO.
All Rights Reserved

Fm7 Bb7 Eb Cm7 Fm7 Bb7 C7
Her with her nose in the air, She has you danc - ing on a string,
Fm7 Bb7 Bb+ Bbm7 Eb9 Bbm7 Eb9 Ab
Break it and she won't care! Won't you take this ad-vice I
Adim Eb Gm Bbm6 C7+ C7-9 Fm7
hand you like a broth - er? Or are you not see-ing things too
p cresc. poco a poco
Abm Eb Gm Bb7 Bbm6 C7-9 Fm7
clear, Are you too much in love to hear, Is it all go-ing in one
Bb7 1. D Eb F9 Fm7 Bb7-9 2. D Eb D Eb
ear and out the oth - er? oth - er?
mf p rall. pp

High Noon

Lyric by Ned Washington
Music by Dimitri Tiomkin

Moderato

Do not for-sake me, oh my dar-lin'

On this our wed-ding day

Do not for-sake me, oh my dar - lin'

Wait _____ wait a - long!

© 1952 and renewed 1980 LARGO MUSIC, INC. and VOLTA MUSIC CORP.
All Rights Reserved

I do not know what fate a-waits me
I on-ly know I must be brave
And I must face a man who hates me
Or lie a cow-ard A cra-ven cow-ard
Or lie a cow-ard in my grave!

Oh, to be torn 'twixt love and du-ty 'spos-in' I lose my fair-haired beau-ty Look at that big hand move a-long_ near-in' HIGH NOON He made a vow while in state's pris-on Vowed it would be my life or his-'n I'm not a-fraid of death but, oh_ what will I do if you leave me? Do not for-sake me, oh my dar-lin'___ You made that prom-ise as a bride___

Fm
Ebdim
Eb
Eb7
Ab
Do not for - sake me, oh my dar - lin'
Al - tho' you're
Eb
Ab
Eb
Ab
Eb
griev - in'
don't think of leav - in'
Now that I need you
Fm7
Bb7
1
Eb
Fm7
2
Eb
by my side!
side!
Wait a -
Ab
Eb
Ab
long
wait a - long
wait a - long
wait a -
Eb
long!
8va
dim
rall.

The Hucklebuck

Words and Music by Roy Alfred and Andy Gibson

Slow Blues Tempo

Here's a dance you should know

When the lights are down low

Grab your ba-by then go.

© 1949 and renewed 1977 BOCA MUSIC, INC.
All Rights Reserved

Chorus

Do THE HUCK-LE BUCK, Do THE HUCK-LE BUCK, if you don't know how to do it Boy, you're out of luck! Push your part-ner out Then you hunch your back Start a lit-tle move-ment in your sac-ro-il-i-ac Wig-gle like a snake Wad-dle like a duck That's the way you do it when you do THE HUCK-LE BUCK

(*Spoken*) Hey! Not now I'll tell you when do THE HUCK-LE BUCK.

I Got It Bad (And That Ain't Good)

Words and Music by Duke Ellington and Paul Francis Webster

Lyrics:

The poets say that all who love are blind; But I'm in love and I know what time it is! The Good Book says "Go seek and ye shall find." Well,

© 1941 and renewed 1968 WEBSTER MUSIC CORP. and SBK/ROBBINS MUSIC
All Rights Reserved

I have sought and my— what a climb it is!— My life is just like the weather It changes with the hours;— When he's near I'm fair and warm-er When he's gone I'm cloud-y with show-ers; in e-mo-tion, like the o-cean it's ei-ther sink or swim— When a wom-an loved a man like I love him.

Moderately slow

Never treats me sweet and gentle the way he should;
Like a lonely weeping willow lost in the wood
I got it bad and that ain't good!

My poor heart is sentimental not made of wood
And the things I tell my pillow no woman should
I got it bad and that ain't good! ⎯⎯⎯ But
I got it bad and that ain't good! ⎯⎯⎯ Tho'

when the week-end's o - ver and Mon - day rolls a - roun' I end up like I
folks with good in - ten - tions tell me to save my tears I'm glad I'm mad a -

start out just cry - in' my heart out He don't love me
bout him I can't live with - out him Lord a - bove me

like I love him no - bod - y could I got it
make him love me the way he should I got it

bad and that ain't good.
bad and that ain't good.

I'll Walk Alone

Lyric by Sammy Cahn
Music by Julie Styne

With feeling

I'll Walk A-lone be-cause to tell you the truth I'll be lone-ly. I don't mind be-ing lone-ly when my heart tells me you are lone-ly too. I'll Walk A-lone they'll ask me

© 1944 and renewed 1972 CAHN MUSIC CO. and MORLEY MUSIC CO., INC.
All Rights Reserved

F6 E7 Am7 D7 F6 E7
why and I'll tell them I'd rath - er; There are dreams I must gath-
A7 D7 G
er, Dreams we fash-ioned the night you held me
Dm7 G7 C Cm
tight. I'll al - ways be near you, wher - ev - er you are Each
Gmaj7 Em7 F#7
night in ev - 'ry prayer. If you call I'll hear you, no

matter how far; just close your eyes and I'll be there. Please walk alone and send your love and your kisses to guide me. Till you're walking beside me, I'll Walk Alone. I'll Walk Alone.

It Started All Over Again

Words by Bill Carey
Music by Carl Fischer

One nev-er knows, does one? How Dan-ny Cu-pid op-er-ates. I know he gave us our walk-ing pa-pers, But here's the in-side sto-ry to date:

© 1942 and renewed 1970 FISCHER-CAREY MUSIC CO. and EMBASSY MUSIC CORP.
All Rights Reserved

REFRAIN

IT START-ED ALL O-VER A-GAIN,___ The mo-ment I looked in your eyes,___

IT START-ED ALL O-VER A-GAIN,___ The thrill we can nev-er dis-guise;___ The

day that we part-ed, so bro-ken heart-ed, Will nev-er re-turn a-gain;___ Dreams I've de-layed,

prom-is-es made, Are start-ing a-new just for you. IT START-ED ALL O-VER A-GAIN,___

87

In The Wee Small Hours Of The Morning

Lyric by Bob Hillard
Music by David Mann

Slowly with restraint

Verse or Interlude
(ad lib)

When the sun is high in the af-ter-noon sky, You can al-ways find some-thing to do. But from dusk till dawn, as the clock ticks on, Some-thing hap-pens to you.

Chorus
(tacet)

IN THE WEE SMALL HOURS_ OF THE MORN-ING,_ While the whole wide world is fast a sleep, You lie a-wake and

© 1955 REDD EVANS MUSIC CO.
All Rights Reserved

think a-bout the girl, (boy,) And nev-er ev-er think of count-ing sheep. When your lone-ly heart has learned its les-son— You'd be her's if on-ly she would call. (his) (he) IN THE WEE SMALL HOURS OF THE MORN-ING,— That's the time you miss her most of all. IN THE (him) time you miss her most of all. (him)

molto rit.

Fine

Intermezzo (A Love Story)

Lyric by Robert Henning
Music by Heinz Provost

Like the dream, you dream to-night, That fades from sight when dark-ness dis-ap-pears, May-be you will van-ish too, The mo-ment when to-mor-row's dawn ap-pears, So my love while stars a-bove in Heav-en's blue Are soft-ly gleam-ing

© 1940 and renewed 1968 EDWARD SCHUBERTH & CO., INC.
By arrangement with Carl Gehrman's Musikforlag, Stockholm, Sweden
All Rights Reserved

I'll dream of you, And I'll live in the glo-ry of your love.

Moderato

When I see the shad-ows fall-ing On a pur-ple sum-mer ev'-ning,

Then is when I hear you call-ing A-cross the lone-ly years,

Oh, how well I still re-mem-ber When an-oth-er sum-mer ev'-ning

One that start-ed out in splen - dor End - ed in tears

Like the dream you dream to-night, That fades from sight when dark-ness dis-ap-

May be cut ✦ to ✦

pears, May-be you will van-ish too, The mo-ment when to-mor-row's dawn ap-

a tempo

pears, So, my love while stars a-bove In Heav-en's blue are soft-ly

beam-ing and gleam-ing, Then I'll live in the glo-ry of your love.

p molto tranquillo

pp morendo

It's Been A Long, Long Time

Lyric by Sammy Cahn
Music by Julie Styne

Slow, with a lift

Nev-er thought that you would be Stand-ing here so close to me. There's so much I feel that I should say But words can wait un-til some oth-er day.

with a lift

© 1945 and renewed 1973 CAHN MUSIC CO. and MORLEY MUSIC CO., INC.
All Rights Reserved

Chorus

Just kiss me once, then kiss me twice, Then kiss me once a-gain,— It's been a long, long time. Have-n't felt like this, my dear, Since can't re-mem-ber when,— It's been a long, long time. You'll nev-er know how man-y dreams I dreamed a-bout you Or just how emp-ty they all seemed with-out you. So, kiss me once, then kiss me twice, Then kiss me once a-gain,___ It's been a long, long time. Just time.

It's Just A Matter Of Time

Words and Music by Clyde Otis, Brook Benton and Belford Hendricks

Moderately with expression

Some-day,— some-way— you'll re-a-lize that you've been blind, Yes, dar-ling,— you're go-ing to need me a-gain, It's Just A Mat-ter Of

© 1958 and renewed 1986 IZA MUSIC CO., TRIO MUSIC CO., INC. and ALLEY MUSIC CORP.
All Rights Reserved

Bb7 A7 Bb7 Eb Ab
Time. Go on, go on until you
Eb Eb7 Ab
reach the end of the line, But I know you'll pass this way again,
F7 Bb7 Eb Ab
It's Just A Mat-ter Of Time. Af-ter I gave you ev-'ry-
Abm Eb Eb7
thing I had, you laughed and called me a clown. Re-mem-ber,

in your search for for-tune and fame, what goes up must come down. I know, I know that one day you'll wake up and find that my love was a true love, It's Just A Mat-ter Of Time. Time.

I've Heard That Song Before

Words and Music by Sammy Cahn and Julie Styne

Moderato *(sweetly)*

It seems to me I've heard that song be-fore;
It's from an old fa-mil-iar score, I know it
well, that mel-o-dy, It's fun-ny

© 1942 and renewed 1969 CAHN MUSIC CO. and MORLEY MUSIC CO., INC.
All Rights Reserved

how a theme recalls a favorite dream, A dream that brought you so close to me. I know each word because I've heard that song before, The lyric said "Forevermore." Forever more's a mem-o-ry. Please have them play it a-gain, And I'll re-mem-ber just when I heard that love-ly song be-fore. It fore.

Java Jive

Words by Milton Drake
Music by Ben Oakland

Lightly, with an easy beat

I love coffee, I love tea, I love the java jive and it loves me.
Coffee and tea and the jivin' and me, a cup, a cup, a cup, a cup, a cup!
I love java, sweet and hot, Whoops! Mister Moto, I'm a coffee pot.

© 1940 and 1968 DRAKE ACTIVITIES and WARNER BROS., INC.
All Rights Reserved

F F/Eb Bb/D Bbm F/C Gm F C7 F F7
Shoot me the pot and I'll pour me a shot, a cup, a cup, a cup, a cup, a cup! Oh,
Bb7 F6
slip me a slug from that won - der-ful mug, and I'll cut a rug, till I'm snug in the jug.
A Drop
Guitar Tacet
Gm7-5 C7
slice of on-ion and a raw one. Draw one.
me a nick-el in my pot, Joe, tak - in' it slow.
Guitar Tacet
Wait-er, wait-er, per - co - la - tor!
F Fdim C7 Gm7 C7 F6 Edim F6
I love cof - fee, I love tea, I love the ja - va jive and it loves me.

105

Cof-fee and tea__ and the jiv-in' and me,__ a cup, a cup, a cup, a cup, a cup.

Bos-ton bean,__ soy bean,__ li-ma bean,__ string bean.__

I'm not keen__ for a bean__ un-less it is a cheer-y cof-fee bean:

D.S. al Coda

CODA

jiv-in' and me,__ a cup, a cup, a cup, a cup, a cup.

Jersey Bounce

Words by Robert B. Wright
Music by Bobby Plater, Tiny Bradshaw and Edward Johnson

Easy Bounce

They call it that JER-SEY BOUNCE___ A rhy-thm that real-ly counts___ The tem-per-ture al-ways mounts___ Where-ev-er they play the fun-ny rhy-thm they play.___ It start-ed on Jour-nal Square.___ And some-bo-dy heard it there___ He

© 1941 and renewed 1968 LEWIS MUSIC PUBLISHING CO., INC.
All Rights Reserved

put it right on the air_____ And now you hear it ev-'ry-where___
Up-town gave it new licks Down-town add-ed some tricks No town
makes it sound the same___ As where it came from! So if you don't feel so hot___
Go out to some Jer-sey spot.___ And wheth-er you're hep or not___
____ The JER-SEY BOUNCE-'ll make you swing.___ They

Love Is All We Need

Words and Music by Ben Raleigh and Don Wolf

Introduction (*Moderately Slow with a beat*)

Love me, love me! Love me, love me!

Love Is All We Need, so won't you take me in your arms and love me, love me!

Love Is All We Need, so darling, press me to your heart and love me, love me!

Tell me we'll always have each other, 'Cause that's all I ever want to know. Tell me you'll always be my

© 1958 and renewed 1986 BEN RALEIGH MUSIC
All Rights Reserved

lov-er,___ 'Cause I will al-ways want you so! Love Is All We Need, so dar-ling, hold me close to you and__ love me, love me! Love Is All We Need to make our ev-'ry dream come true, So__ love me, love me! All we ev-er, ev-er need is

1. love!
2. love.

Mairzy Doats

Words and Music by Milton Drake, Al Hoffman and Jerry Livingston

Lightly

I know a dit-ty nut-ty as a fruit cake, goof-y as a goon and sil-ly as a loon.

Some call it pret-ty, oth-ers call it cra-zy, but they all sing this tune:

Mair-zy doats and do-zy doats and lid-dle lam-zy div-ey, a kid-dle-y div-ey too, would-n't you? Yes!

© 1943 and renewed 1971 DRAKE ACTIVITIES, AL HOFFMAN SONGS and HALLMARK MUSIC CO., INC.
All Rights Reserved

Mair-zy doats and do-zy doats and lid-dle lam-zy div-ey, a kid-dle-y div-y too, would-n't you? If the words sound queer, and fun-ny to your ear, a lit-tle bit jum-bled and jiv-ey, Sing "Mares eat oats and does eat oats and lit-tle lambs eat i-vy." Oh! Mair-zy doats and do-zy doats and lid-dle lam-zy div-ey, a kid-dle-y div-ey too, would-n't you? A kid-dle-y div-ey too, would-n't you?

May You Always

Words and Music by Larry Markes and Dick Charles

Moderately

MAY YOU AL-WAYS walk in sun-shine, slum-ber warm when night winds blow. MAY YOU AL-WAYS live with laugh-ter for a smile be-comes you so. May good for-tune find your door-way, may the blue-bird sing your song. May no trou-ble trav-el your way, may no wor-ry stay too long.

© 1958 and renewed 1986 HEARTLY MUSIC CO.
All Rights administered by September Music Corp.
All Rights Reserved

May your heart-aches be for-got-ten, may no tears be spilled. May old ac-quain-tance be re-mem-bered, and your cup of kind-ness filled, and MAY YOU AL-WAYS be a dream-er, may your wild-est dream come true. May you find some-one to love, as much as I love you. you.

Midnight Sun

Words and Music by Johnny Mercer, Sonny Burke and Lionel Hampton

Slowly, with a beat

Your lips were like a red and ruby chalice, warmer than the summer night_____ The clouds were like an alabaster palace rising to a snowy height._____ Each

I can't explain the silver rain that found me, or was that a moonlight veil?_____ The music of the universe around me, or was that a nightingale?_____ And

flame of it may dwindle to an ember, and the stars forget to shine,_____ And we may see the meadow in December, icy white and crystalline._____ But

© 1947, 1954 and renewed 1975, 1982 CRYSTAL MUSIC PUBLISHERS, INC.
All Rights Reserved

star its own au-ro-ra bo-re-a-lis, sud-den-ly you held me tight,
then your arms mi-rac-u-lous-ly found me, sud-den-ly the sky turned pale,
oh my dar-ling al-ways I'll re-mem-ber when your lips were close to mine,

I could see the Mid-night Sun.
I could see the Mid-night Sun.
And we saw the Mid-night Sun.

Was there such a night, it's a thrill I still don't quite be-lieve, But af-ter you were gone, there was still some star-dust on my sleeve. The

Misirlou

English Lyric by Fred Wise, Milton Leeds and S.K. Russell
Spanish Lyric by J. Pina
Title and Music by N. Roubanis

Des-ert shad-ows creep a-cross pur-ple sands
Cuan-do a-le-gre tu son-ries mu-jer

Na-tives kneel in prayer by their car-a-vans
De-jan-do tu a-mor res-plan-de-cer

There sil-hou-et-ted
Aun-que quie-ra ol-vi-

© 1941 and renewed 1969 MISIRLOU MUSIC, INC.
All Rights Reserved

un-der an east-ern star
dar-te nun-ca po - dre

I see my long lost blos-som of Shal-i- mar
Tie-nes a-pris-ion-a-do to-do mi ser

CHORUS

You / Oh — MI - SIR - LOU / MI - SIR - LOU

Are the moon and the sun Fair-est
Del o-ri - en - te la flor eres

one _____ Old Tem-ple Bells are
tu _____ Tu mi - rar es des-

call-ing a - cross the sand _____
te - llo de ins-pi - ra - ción _____

We'll find our Kis-met an-swer-ing love's com-mand _____
Que de-ja em-be - le - za-do mi co - ra - zon _____

You _____ MI-SIR-LOU _____ Are a
Cuan - - to do - lor _____ si es que in-

Eb
Eb7
D
dream of de - light In the night
gra - ta tu nie - gas mi a - mor
molto cresc.
ff
D
To an o - a - sis sprin - kled by stars a - bove
Ju - ro nun - ca ven - gar - me de tu trai - cion
marc.
Gmi
Heav - en will guide us Al - lah will bless our love
Aun - que vi - va en el mun - do sin co - ra - zon
p
Gmi
Eb7
D
Gmi
Ah Ah MI - SIR - LOU
Ah Ah MI - SIR - LOU
p
mf
rit.
espr.
morendo
f-p

My Foolish Heart

Words by Ned Washington
Music by Victor Young

Slowly and expressively

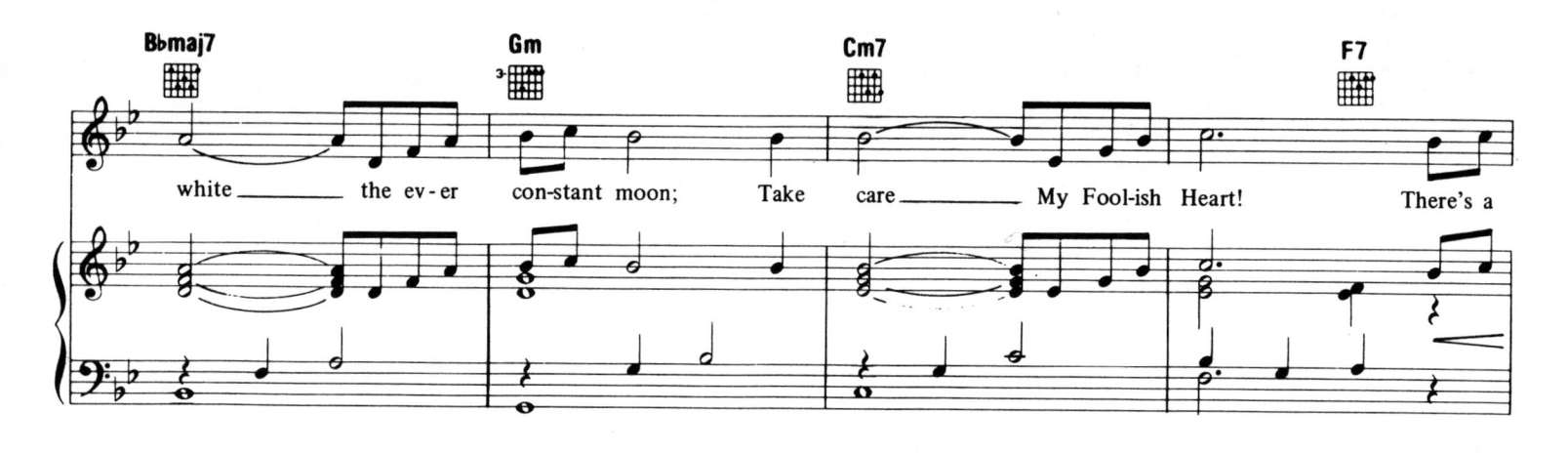

The night is like a lovely tune, Beware My Foolish Heart! How white the ever constant moon; Take care My Foolish Heart! There's a line between love and fascination that's hard to see on an evening such as this, For they both give the very same sensation when you're lost in the magic of a kiss. {His} {Her}

© 1949 and renewed 1977 LARGO MUSIC, INC. and WARNER/CHAPPELL MUSIC
All Rights Reserved

Bb Gm Cm7 Adim Bbmaj7
lips are much too close to mine, Be - ware My Fool-ish Heart But should our ea-ger
Gm Cm7 D7+5 D7 D7-5 D7 Gm Gm7
lips com-bine Then let the fire start For this time it is - n't fas - ci -
Gb9 Gb7 Bb Dm7-5 G7 Cm7
na - tion, or a dream that will fade and fall a - part, It's love this time, it's
F9 Cm7 F7-9 1 Bb Gm7 Cm7 F7 2 Bb Gm7 Cm7 Cb7 Bb6
love, My Fool - ish Heart. The heart.
mp
rall.

Nature Boy

Words and Music by Eden Ahbez

Slowly

With a Jazz feel

There was a boy, _____ A ver-y strange, en-chant-ed boy;

They say he wan-dered ver-y far, ver-y far

O-ver land and sea. A lit-tle shy _____

© 1948 and renewed 1976 GOLDEN WORLD
All Rights Reserved

and sad of eye,_____ But very wise_____ was he._____

And then one day,_____ one summer day, he passed my way

And as we spoke of many things, fools and kings,

This he said to me: "The great-est thing you'll ev-er learn Is just to love and be loved in re-turn". There

just to love and be loved in re-turn".

The Old Lamplighter

Words by Charles Tobias
Music by Nat Simon

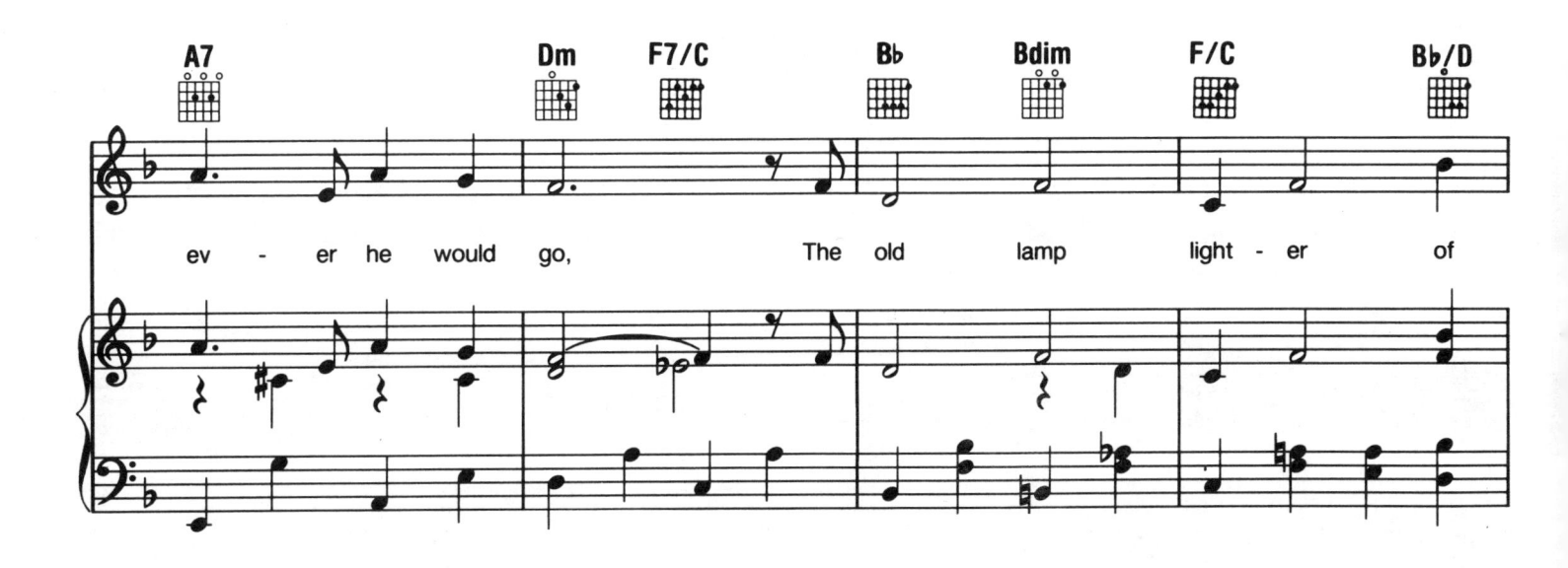

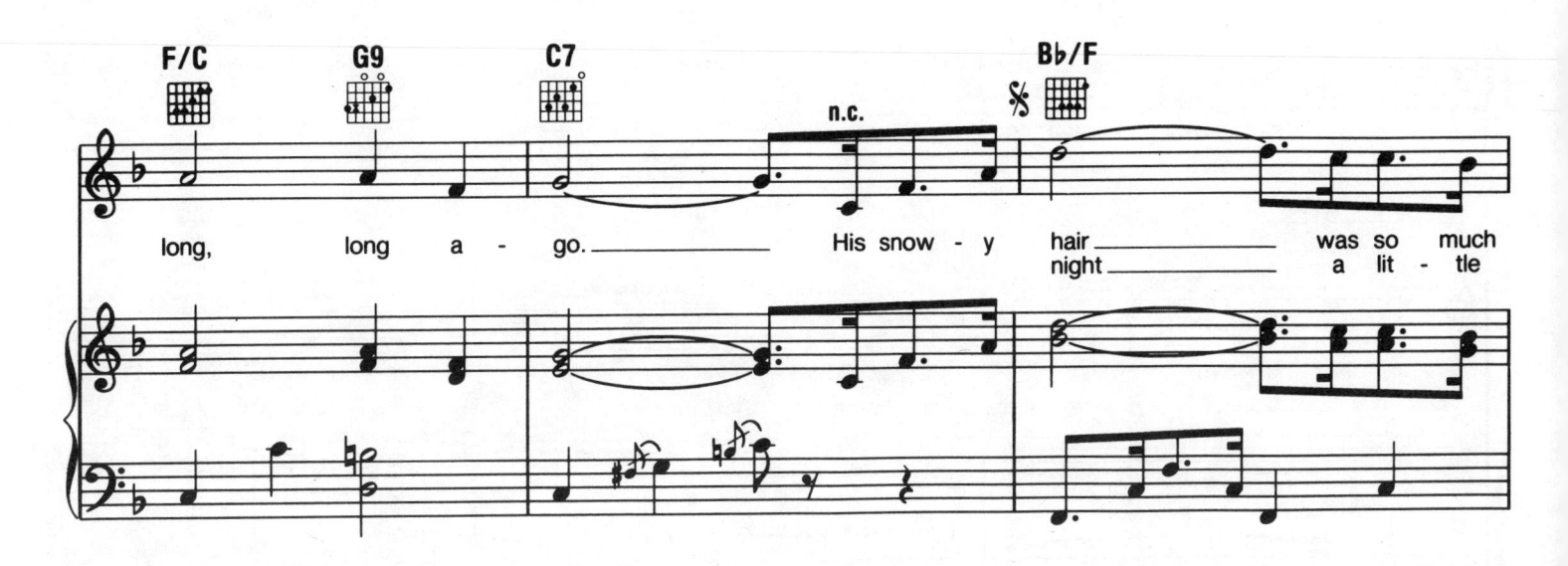

He made the night a little brighter wherever he would go, The old lamplighter of long, long ago. His snowy hair was so much night a little

© 1946 and renewed 1974 CHED MUSIC CORP. and HARRY VON TILZER MUSIC PUBLISHING CO.
All Rights Reserved

whit - er be - neath the can - dle glow, The old lamp -
bright - er wher - ev - er he would go, The old lamp -

light - er of long, long a - go. You'd hear the
light - er of long, long a - go. Now if you

pat - ter of his feet as he came tod - dling down the street, His smile would hide a lone - ly heart you
look up at the sky you'll un - der - stand the rea - son why The lit - tle stars at night are all a-

see. If there were sweet - hearts in the park he'd pass a lamp and leave it dark Re -

mem - ber - ing the days that used to be. For he re - calls when dreams were new, he loved some - one who loved him too Who walks with him a - lone in mem - o - ry. He made the

D.S. al Coda

CODA

glow. He turns them on when night is here, he turns them off when dawn is here, The lit - tle man we loved of long a - go.

Night Train

Words by Oscar Washington and Lewis C. Simpkins
Music by Jimmy Forrest

Slow Blues Tempo

Night train, that took my baby so far away,
Night train, your whistle tore my poor heart in two,
Night train, please bring my baby back home to me;

Night train, that took my baby so far away,
Night train, your whistle tore my poor heart in two;
Night train, please bring my baby back home to me;

Tell her I love her more and more ev'ry day.
She's gone, and I don't know what I'm gonna do!
She's gone; the blues she left just won't set me free.

My mother said I'd lose her if I ever did abuse her, should have listened. My

© 1952 and renewed 1980 FREDERICK MUSIC CO.
All Rights Reserved

mother said I'd lose her if I ever did abuse her, should have listened. Now

I have learned my lesson, my sweet baby was a blessin', should have listened.

It's blue Monday morning she left me last Saturday night; Now it's blue Monday morning; She left me last Saturday night; Ev'ry time I hear trains blow I get the blues; Can't sleep at night.

Nina Never Knew

Words by Milton Drake
Music by Louis Alter

Slowly

Girls were made to kiss, but Ni-na Nev-er Knew.

Girls are born for this, but Ni-na Nev-er Knew.

Sweet sur-prise filled Ni-na's eyes; she did not un-der-stand,

© 1952 and renewed 1980 LOUIS ALTER MUSIC and DRAKE ACTIVITIES
All Rights Reserved

131

When I kissed her hand, why dreams be-gan to stir deep down in-side of her!
When I whis-pered things that Ni-na nev-er heard, Ni-na's heart took
wings with ev-'ry ten-der word. Then sud-den-ly she clung to me; she
learned to love some-how. And I'm so glad that Ni-na Nev-er Knew till
now. _____ now. _____

Orange Colored Sky

Words and Music by Milton DeLugg and Willie Stein

you. One look and I yelled "Tim-ber Watch out for fly-ing glass" 'Cause the ceil-ing fell in, and the bot-tom fell out, I went in-to a spin, and I start-ed to shout "I've been hit! This is it! This is it!" I was walk-in' a-long Mind-in' my busi-ness when Violent love came and hit me in the eye. Flash! Bam! A-la-ka-zam! Out of an O-RANGE COLORED SKY. I was O-range col-ored, Pur-ple striped, Pret-ty green Pol-ka dot-ted sky Flash! Bam! A-la-ka-zam! and good-bye.

Paper Doll

Words and Music by Johnny S. Black

Slowly

I guess I've had a million dolls or more, I guess I've played the doll game o'er and o'er, I just quar-reled with Sue,— That's why I'm blue;— She's gone a-way and left me just like all dolls do. I'll tell you boys it's tough to be a-

© 1991 PORTSIDE MUSIC (ASCAP)
All Rights Reserved

lone And it's tough to love a doll that's not your own. I'm thru with all of them,

I'll nev-er fall a-gain, 'Cause this is what I'll do.

I'm goin' to buy a Pa-per Doll that I can call my own, A

doll that oth-er fel-lows can-not steal And then the flir-ty, flir-ty guys with their

C A7 E♭dim G7 C7 Cdim C7
flir - ty, flir - ty eyes, Will have to flirt with dol - lies that are real. When
F D7 G7 C7 F F D7 G7 C7
I come home at night she will be wait - ing, She'll be the tru - est doll in all this
A7 Dm6 A7 B♭ Bdim F A7 D7
world. I'd rath - er have a Pa - per Doll to call my own, than have a
G7 B♭m6 C7 F A♭dim C7 F
fick - le - mind - ed real live girl. I'm goin' to girl.
1
2

Peg O' My Heart

Words by Alfred Bryan
Music by Fred Fischer

Slowly

Verse:

I grow tired of a song __ If it lin-gers too long __ And ros-es I've plucked __ and thrown a-
Oh! my heart's in a whirl. __ O-ver one lit-tle girl, __ I love her, I love __ her, yes, I

way __ But still I nev-er change my tune __ When we are stroll-ing 'neath the
do, __ Al-tho' her heart is far a-way, __ I hope to make her mine some

moon __ Pret-ty Peg can't you see __ heav-en sent you to me __ I
day. __ Ev-'ry beau-ti-ful rose, __ Ev-'ry vi-o-let knows, __ I

© 1989 PORTSIDE MUSIC (ASCAP)
All Rights Reserved

need you much more than I can say, I know I'm aim-ing high But a
love her, I love her fond and true, And her heart fond-ly sighs, As I

dream-er can try So why can't I Just dream and sigh my love song!
sing to her eyes, Her eyes of blue, Sweet eyes of blue, my dar-ling!

Refrain: *Slowly*

Peg O' My Heart I love you, Don't let us part,
Peg O' My Heart I love you, We'll nev-er part,

I love you, I al-ways knew, It would be you,
I love you, Dear lit-tle girl, Sweet lit-tle girl,

Since I heard your lilt-ing laugh-ter, It's your I-rish heart I'm af-ter, Peg O' My Heart,
Sweet-er than the Rose of Er-in, are your win-ning smiles en-dear-in', Peg O' My Heart,
Your glanc-es make my heart say "How's chanc-es?"
Your glanc-es with I-rish art en-trance us,
Come, be my own— Come, make your home in my heart.
Come, be my own— Come, make your home in my heart.

Please Mr. Sun

Words by Sid Frank
Music by Ray Getzov

Slowly, with expression

Talk to {him, her,} PLEASE, MISTER SUN, Speak to {him, her,} Mister Rainbow, And take {him, her} under your branches, Mister Tree.

Whisper to {him, her,} Mister Wind, Sing to {him, her,} Mister Robin, And Missus Moonlight, Put in a word for me.

© 1951 and renewed 1979 WEISS & BARRY COPYRIGHTS, INC.
All Rights Reserved

141

Pretend

Words and Music by Lew Douglas, Cliff Parman and Frank Lavere

PRE-TEND you're hap-py when you're blue. It is-n't ver-y hard to do, and you'll find hap-pi-ness with-out an end, when ev-er you PRE-TEND. Re-mem-ber, an-y-one can dream, and noth-ing's bad as it may seem. The lit-tle things you have-n't

© 1952 and renewed 1980 BRANDOM MUSIC CO.
All Rights Reserved

got, could be a lot, if you'd PRE - TEND. You'll find a love you can share, one you can call all your own. Just close your eyes, {she'll / he'll} be there. You'll nev-er be a-lone. And if you sing this mel-o-dy, you'll be pre-tend-ing, just like me. The world is mine, it can be yours, my friend, So why don't you PRE-TEND. PRE-TEND you're hap-py when you're TEND.

Que Sera, Sera (Whatever Will Be, Will Be)

Words and Music by Jay Livingston and Ray Evans

Medium Waltz Tempo

1. When I was just a lit-tle girl, I asked my moth-er, "What will I be? Will I be pret-ty? Will I be rich?" Here's what she said to me:
2. just a child in school, I asked my teach-er, "What should I try? Should I paint pic-tures? Should I sing songs?" This was her wise re-ply:
3. up and fell in love, I asked my {lov-er / sweet-heart}, "What lies a-head? Will we have rain-bows day af-ter day?" Here's what my {lov-er / sweet-heart} said:
4. child-ren of my own, They ask their {moth-er / fath-er}, "What will I be? Will I be {pret-ty? / hand-some?} Will I be rich?" I tell them ten-der-ly:

© 1955 and renewed 1983 by Jay Livingston and Ray Evans
Assigned 1984 to JAY LIVINGSTON MUSIC CORP. and ST. ANGELO MUSIC CORP.
All Rights Reserved

REFRAIN
F
C
"Que Se - ra, Se - ra, What - ev - er Will Be will be;
mf
G7
C
The fu - ture's not ours to see. Que Se - ra, Se - ra!
Dm7 G7 Dm7 G7 C
1, 2, 3.
Guitar tacet
What will be will be!"
2. When I was
3. When I grew
4. When I have
C Dm G7 C F C
4.
Que Se - ra, Se - ra!"
p
8va bassa

Rags To Riches

Words and Music by Richard Adler and Jerry Ross

I know I'd go from RAGS TO RICH-ES,— If you would on-ly say you care!

And tho' my pock-et may be emp-ty I'd be a mil-lion-aire!

My clothes may still be torn and tat-tered But in my heart I'd be a king,

© 1953 and renewed 1981 RICHARD ADLER MUSIC and J.J. ROSS CO.
All Rights Reserved

Your love is all that ev-er mat-tered,— It's ev-'ry-thing!—— So o-pen your arms and you'll o-pen the door to all the trea-sures that I'm hop-ing for, Hold me and kiss me and tell me you're mine ev-er-more! Must I for-ev-er stay a beg-gar?— Whose gold-en dream will not come true, or will I go from RAGS TO RICH-ES?— My fate is up to you! you!

(Get Your Kicks On) Route 66

Words and Music by Bobby Troup

Medium Jazz 4

© 1946 and renewed 1974 LONDONTOWN MUSIC
All Rights Reserved

F6 Bb9 E F6
winds from Chi - ca - go to L. A., more than
f mf
Bb9 F6 Gm7
two thou-sand miles all the way. Get your kicks on
f
C13 F F13 Eb13 C13 F/C
Route Six - ty - Six! Now you go thru Saint Loo-ey
f
Bb9 F/C F7 Bb9
Jop - lin, Mis-sour - i and Ok - la - hom-a Cit - y is might - y pret - ty. You'll see Am-ar -
mf
F6/9 F Bdim F Gm7 C7
il - lo, Gal - lup, New Mex - i - co; Flag - staff, Ar - i - zon - a;
f

Gm7 C7 Dm7/C Cdim C9sus C7
don't for - get Wi - no - na, King - man, Bar - stow, San Ber - nar - din - o. Won't
mp cresc.
f
mf
F6 Bb9 E F6
you get hip to this time - ly tip: When you
f
mf
Bb9 F6
make that Cal - i - for - nia trip. Get your
f
mf
Gm7 C13 1 F D7 C#7 C7 C11 2 F Gm7 G#dim
kicks on Route Six - ty - Six! If you
mf
f
F Gm7 C13 F E13 F13
Get your kicks on Route Six - ty - Six!
dim.
p
f

Shoo Fly Pie And Apple Pan Dowdy

Words by Sammy Gallop
Music by Guy Wood

Slow bounce

If you wan-na do right by your ap-pe-tite,— If you're fus-sy a-bout your food,— Take a choo-choo to-day, head New Eng-land way,— and we'll put you in the hap-pi-est mood,— with:—

© 1945 and renewed 1973 SAMMY GALLOP MUSIC
All Rights Reserved

F Bb C7 F Bdim C7
Shoo-Fly Pie And Ap-ple Pan Dow-dy makes your eyes light up, Your tum-my say "how-dy,"
mp-mf
sf
F Bb F Bb F F6
Shoo-Fly Pie And Ap-ple Pan Dow-dy, I nev-er get e-nough of that won-der-ful stuff.
F Bb C7 F Bdim C7
Shoo-Fly Pie And Ap-ple Pan Dow-dy makes the sun come out when Heav-ens are cloud-y,
sf
F Bb F Bb F F6
Shoo-Fly Pie And Ap-ple Pan Dow-dy, I nev-er get e-nough of that won-der-ful stuff!

A7
D9
G7
Ma-ma! when you bake, Ma-ma! I don't want cake; Ma-ma!
f
C7
Cdim
Gm7
C7
F
for my sake go to the o-ven and make some ev-er-lov-in' sh, Shoo-Fly Pie And
3
ff
p
Bb
C7
F
Bdim
C7
F
Ap-ple Pan Dow-dy makes your eyes light up, Your 'tum-my' say "how-dy," Shoo Fly Pie And
sf
Bb
F
Bb
1
F
F6
2
F
F6
Ap-ple Pan Dow-dy I nev-er get e-nough of that won-der-ful stuff! won-der-ful stuff!

See You In September

Words and Music by Sid Wayne and Sherman Edwards

VERSE: I'll be a-lone each and ev-'ry night, While you're a-way, don't for-get to write.

REFRAIN: SEE YOU IN SEP-TEM-BER, See you when the sum-mer's thru. Here we are, say-ing good-bye at the sta-tion, Sum-mer va-ca-tion is tak-ing you a-way. Have a

© 1959 and renewed 1987 HOLLY HILL MUSIC and KEITH-VALERIE MUSIC CORP.
All Rights Reserved

good time, _____ but re-mem-ber _____ There is dan-ger _____ in the sum-mer moon a-bove; _____ Will I SEE YOU _____ IN SEP-TEM-BER, _____ Or lose you _____ to a sum-mer love? _____

INTERLUDE

Count-ing the days 'til I'll be with you, Count-ing the hours and the min-utes too. Have a

D.S. al Coda

CODA

_____ Or lose you _____ to a sum-mer love? _____

Sincerely

Words and Music by Harvey Fuqua and Alan Freed

Slowly (with a good beat)

Sin - cer - ly, _____ Oh! ___ Yes, ___ Sin - cere - ly, 'Cause I love you so ___ dear - ly, ___ Please say ___ you'll be mine. ___ Sin -

© 1954 and renewed 1982 LIAISON II PUBLISHING CO.
All Rights Reserved

157

158

Somewhere Along The Way

Words by Sammy Gallop
Music by Kurt Adams

Slowly (*with much feeling*)

Verse

Here am I with-out you, Lost with-out your warm em-brace.

Still so mad a-bout you, And won-d'ring who took my place.

Chorus (*Very slowly*)

I used to walk with you a-long the av-en-ue, Our hearts were care-free and gay.

© 1952 and renewed 1980 SAMMY GALLOP MUSIC and MUSIC SALES CORPORATION
All Rights Reserved

How could I know I'd lose you, SOME-WHERE A-LONG THE WAY.

The friends we used to know, would al-ways smile, "Hel-lo." No love like our love, they'd say.

Then love slipped thru our fin-gers, SOME-WHERE A-LONG THE WAY. I should for-get, but with the lone-li-ness of night, I start re-mem-ber-ing ev'ry-thing. You're gone, and yet ___ there's still a feel-ing deep in-side _ that you will al-ways be,

part of me. So now I look for you, _ a-long the av-en-ue, _

And as I wan-der I pray, That some-day soon I'll find you,

1. SOME-WHERE A-LONG THE WAY.

2. SOME-WHERE A-LONG THE WAY.

Tammy

Words and Music by Jay Livingston and Ray Evans

Moderately

Refrain - Tenderly

1. I hear the cot-ton-woods whis-p'rin' a-bove:
2. Whip-poor-will, whip-poor-will, you and I know,

Tam-my! Tam-my! Tam-my's {my / in} love! The ole hoot-ie
Tam-my! Tam-my! Can't let him go! The breeze from the

owl hoot-ie-hoo's to the dove: Tam-my! Tam-my!
bay-ou keeps mur-mur-ing low: Tam-my! Tam-my!

© 1956 and renewed 1984 by Jay Livingston and Ray Evans
Assigned to JAY LIVINGSTON MUSIC CORP. and ST. ANGELO MUSIC CORP.
All Rights Reserved

Bb9 Bb7b9 Eb (Tacet) Eb Ab F F7
Tam-my's {my / in} love! Does my {dar - ling / lov - er} feel what I feel when {she / he} comes
You love him so! When the night is warm, soft and warm, I long for his
cresc. poco a poco
Bb Bb7 G G7 Cm Ab Eb Gm Cm
near? My heart beats so joy - ful - ly, you'd think that {she / he} could
charms! I'd sing like a vi - o - lin if I were in his
mf
Fm7 Bb7 Eb Gm Ab Eb
hear! Wish I knew if {she / he} knew what I'm dream - ing of!
arms! Wish I knew if he knew what I'm dream - ing of!
mp
Cm Gm Bb7 1. Eb Adim Bb7 2. Eb
Tam - my! Tam - my! Tam - my's {my / in} love!
Tam - my! Tam - my! Tam - my's in love!
mp
mp
rit.

This Could Be The Start Of Something Big

Words and Music by Steve Allen

Brightly, with spirit

1. You're walk-ing a - long the street, or you're at a par-ty,
2. You're do - in' your in - come tax, or buy - in' a tooth-brush,

Or else you're a - lone and then you sud - den - ly dig;
Or hur - ry - in' home be - cause the ho - ur is late;

You're look - in' in some - one's eyes, you sud - den - ly re - al - ize
Then sud - den - ly there you go, the ver - y next thing you know,

© 1956 and renewed 1984 ROSEMEADOW PUBLISHING CORP.
All Rights Reserved

That **THIS COULD BE THE START OF SOME-THING** big!
Is **THIS COULD BE THE START OF SOME-THING** great!

You're lunch-ing at "Twen-ty One" and watch-ing your di-et,
You're hav-in' a snow-ball fight, or pick-in' up dai-sies,

De-clin-ing a Char-lotte Russe, ac-cept-ing a fig;
You're sing-in' a hap-py tune, or knock-in' on wood;

When out of a clear blue sky, it's sud-den-ly gal and guy,
When all of a sud-den you look up and there's some-one new,

And **THIS COULD BE THE START OF SOME-THING** big!
Oh, **THIS COULD BE THE START OF SOME-THING** good!

There's no con-trol-ling the un-roll-ing of your fate, my friend, ___ Who knows what's writ-ten in the mag-ic book? But when a lov-er you dis-cov-er at the gate, my friend, ___ In-vite {her}{him} in with-out a sec-ond look! You're up in an aer-o-plane, ___ or din-ing at

Your des-tined lov-er you'll dis-cov-er in a fright-'ning flash, ___ So keep your heart a-wake both night and day, Be-cause the meet-ing may be fleet-ing as a light-'ning flash ___ And you don't want to let it slip a-way! You're watch-ing the sun come up, ___ or count-ing your

Fm7 Bb7 Fm C+ Fm7 Bb7
Sar - di's, Or ly - ing at Mal - i - bu, a - lone on the
mon - ey, Or else in a dim ca - fé, you're or - der - ing
Cm Eb+ Cm7 Cm6 Ab Adim
sand; You sud - den - ly hear a bell and right a - way
wine; Then sud - den - ly there {she he} is, you want to be
Gm Fm Gb C9 Fm7 Bb7 Fm7 Bb7
you can tell, That THIS COULD BE THE START OF SOME-THING
where {she he} is, And this must be the start of some - thing,
1. Ebdim Ebdim Bb7 2. Ebmaj7 C7-9
grand! 2.You're do - in' your This could be the heart of some - thing,
mf
Fm C+ Fm7 Bb7 Eb
(opt.)
THIS COULD BE THE START OF SOME-THING fine!
sf

'Tis Autumn

Words and Music by Henry Nemo

Moderately Slow

You tell me I'm act-ing sil-ly, I'm not sil-ly, just chil-ly, mm

You say I'm prov-ing my-self a goof, For what I say or do I've the ab-so-lute proof:

Rit.   a tempo

Refrain

Ole Fath-er Time checked so there'd be no doubt;
trees say they're tired, they've borne too much fruit;

© 1941 and renewed 1969 INDANO MUSIC CO.
All Rights Reserved

Called on the north wind to come on out, then cupped his hands so
Charmed all the way-side, there's no dis-pute. Now, shed-ding leaves, they

proud-ly to shout___ La-de-da-de-da-de dum,___ 'TIS AU-TUMN.___ The
don't give a hoot,___ La-de-da-de-da-de dum___ 'TIS

AU-TUMN.___ Then the birds got to-geth-er to chirp a-bout the weath-er___ Mmm___

Af-ter mak-ing their de-cis-ion in

bird-y like pre-cis-ion, turned a-bout and made a bee-line to the south. My hold-ing you close real-ly is no crime, ask the birds, the trees and Ole Fath-er Time. It's just to help the mer-cu-ry climb La-de-da-de-da-de dum 'TIS AU-TUMN.

you. Hold me close, nev-er let me go; Hold me close, melt my heart like A-pril snow. I'll love you till the blue-bells for-get to bloom, I'll love you till the clo-ver has lost it's per-

The Twelfth Of Never

Words by Paul Francis Webster
Music by Jerry Livingston

Very Slowly, with feeling

You ask how much I need you, must I ex-plain? I need you, oh, my dar-ling, like ros-es need rain. You ask how long I'll love you, I'll tell you true, Un-til The Twelfth Of Nev-er, I'll still be lov-ing

© 1956 and renewed 1984 HALLMARK MUSIC CO., INC.
All Rights Reserved

fume. I'll love you till the po-ets run out of rhyme, Un-til The Twelfth Of Nev-er, And that's a long, long time; Un-til The Twelfth Of Nev-er, And that's a long, long time. You that's a long, long time.

Two Different Worlds

Lyric by Sid Wayne
Music by Al Frisch

Broadly

Two Dif-f'rent Worlds, _____ we live in Two Dif-f'rent Worlds, _____ for we've been told that a love like ours could nev-er be. _____ So far a-part, _____ they say we're so far a-part _____ and that we have-n't the right to change our des-tin-y. _____ When will they learn _____ that a heart does-n't

© 1956 and renewed 1984 HOLLY HILL MUSIC and MYRA MUSIC
All Rights Reserved

175

draw a line._____ Noth-ing mat-ters if I am yours_____ and you are mine._____ Two Dif-f'rent Worlds,_____ we live in Two Dif-f'rent Worlds,_____ but we will show them, as we walk to-geth-er in the sun,_____ that our Two Dif-f'rent Worlds,_____ are one._____

Wake The Town And Tell The People

Words by Sammy Gallop
Music by Jerry Livingston

Moderato

Verse (ad lib)

They stood there in the moon-light, She sighed and spoke his name; He looked up from her kiss-es Just long e-nough to ex-claim:

Refrain (Moderately, With A Lilt)

WAKE THE TOWN AND TELL THE PEO-PLE___ Sing it to the moon a-bove,___

© 1954 and renewed 1982 SAMMY GALLOP MUSIC and HALLMARK MUSIC CO., INC.
All Rights Reserved

WAKE THE TOWN AND TELL THE PEO-PLE___ tell 'em that we're so in love___

Let's be-gin the cel-e-bra-tion,___ let's de-clare a hol-i-day___

Send a wed-ding in-vi-ta-tion to the neigh-bors right a-way.___

When you are close to me___ and my heart is danc-ing with de-light___

C7 C G7 C7 F Am Am7 D7 Dm7
— I want the world to see — heav - en in my arms to - night. —
G7 C G9
— Shout it from the high - est stee - ple — ring the bells the whole night through —
Ped.
G9
— WAKE THE TOWN AND TELL THE PEO - PLE — Tell them I'm in love with
1. C C♯dim Dm7 G7
you — WAKE THE TOWN AND TELL THE
2. C
you. —
l. h.
rall.

When The Swallows Come Back To Capistrano

Words and Music by Leon Rene

tenderly

WHEN THE SWAL-LOWS COME BACK___ TO CAP - I - STRAN - O,___

___ that's the day___ you prom-ised to___ come back to

© 1940 and renewed 1967 LEON RENE PUBLICATIONS
All Rights Reserved

me._____ When you whis-pered fare-well_____ in Cap-i-stran-o,_____ 'twas the day_____ the swal-lows flew out to the sea._____

All the mis-sion bells will ring, the chap-el choir will sing.
While the al-tar can-dles burn, my heart is burn-ing too,

The hap-pi-ness you'll
If you should not re-

bring will live in my mem-o-ry.
turn I'll still be wait-ing for you. WHEN THE

SWAL-LOWS COME BACK TO CAP-I-STRAN-O,

that's the day I pray that you'll come back to

1. me. WHEN THE
2. me.

We'll Be Together Again

Lyric by Frankie Lane
Music by Carl Fischer

Verse ad lib.

Here in our moment of darkness,— Remember the sun has shone;
Laugh and the world will laugh with you, Cry, and you cry a-lone.

Chorus, Slowly with expression

No tears, no fears,— Remember there's always to-mor-row,— So what if we have to part, WE'LL BE TO-GETH-ER A-GAIN. Your

© 1945 and renewed 1973 FISCHER-CAREY MUSIC CO. and CARES MUSIC
All Rights Reserved

kiss, your smile ___ Are mem-'ries I'll treas-ure for - ev - er, ___ So try think-ing with your heart, WE'LL BE TO-GETH-ER A-GAIN.

Times when I know you'll be lone-some, ___ Times when I know you'll be sad; Don't let temp-ta-tion sur-round you, ___ Don't let the blues make you bad; Some-day, some way, ___ We both have a life-time be-fore us, ___ For part-ing is not good-bye, WE'LL BE TO-GETH-ER A-GAIN. No GAIN.

Who Wouldn't Love You

Words by Bill Carey
Music by Carl Fischer

Rather slowly

You're won-der-ful,— you're mar-vel-ous, You're the lov-li-est girl I know— You're sim-ply dev-as-tat-ing, cap-ti-vat-ing, No won-der I love you so;—

© 1942 and renewed 1970 FISCHER-CAREY MUSIC CO.
All Rights Reserved

CHORUS

Who would-n't love you, Who would-n't care

You're so en-chant-ing People must stare

You're the dream that dream-ers want to dream a-bout

You're the breath of spring that lov-ers ga a-bout, are mad a-bout

Who Wouldn't Love You, Who wouldn't buy the west-side of heaven If you winked your eye. You're the answer to my ev'ry prayer, darling, *Who Wouldn't Love You*, Who wouldn't care.

Who wouldn't care.

Wonderful! Wonderful!

Words by Ben Raleigh
Music by Sherman Edwards

Sometimes we walk hand in hand by the sea And we breathe in the cool salt-y air; You turn to me with a kiss in your eyes And my heart feels a thrill be-yond com-pare! Then your lips cling to mine, it's

Sometimes we stand on the top of a hill And we gaze at the earth and the sky; I turn to you and you melt in my arms, There we are, dar-ling, on-ly you and I! What a mo-ment to share, it's

© 1955 and renewed 1983 KEITH-VALERIE MUSIC CORP., a division of Music Sales Corporation
and PIEDMONT MUSIC COMPANY
All Rights Reserved

Cm7 3fr. B°7 3fr. Cm D° Ebm6
1. Bb C9 F7
WON - DER - FUL! WON-DER-FUL! Oh, so won - der - ful, my love!
WON - DER - FUL! WON-DER-FUL!
2. Bb Cm7 3fr. F7 3fr. 3fr. Bb Cm7 C#°7 Bb Ebmaj7 Eb6 Fm7 Bb7
Oh, so won-der-ful, my love! This world is full of won-d'rous things, it's
Eb Gm7 3fr. Eb6 C7 F7
true, But they would-n't have much mean-ing with-out you.
Bb6 Eb6 Bb6 Eb6 Bb6 Eb6
Some qui - et eve - nings I sit by your side And we're lost in a world of our

Bb6 Eb6 Ab6 4fr. Eb6 Ab6 4fr.
own; I feel the glow of your un - spo - ken love, I'm a -
Eb Cm7 3fr. Am7-5 D7 Gm 3fr. G7
ware of the treas - ure that I own. And I say to my - self, it's
Cm7 3fr. Bo7 3fr. Cm Do Ebm6 Bb Cm7 3fr. F7
WON - DER - FUL! WON - DER - FUL! Oh, so won - der - ful, my love!
1. Bb Bb6 Eb6
D. S. al Fine
2. Bb Bb6 Eb6 Bb Bb6 Eb6 Bb
love!
Fine
dim.
pp
Fine

Why Don't You Believe Me

Words and Music by Lew Douglas, Kim Laney and Roy Rodde

Slowly

WHY DON'T YOU BE-LIEVE ME   It's you I a-dore

For-ev-er and ev-er   Can I prom-ise more?

I've told you so oft-en   The way that I care

© 1952 and renewed 1980 BRANDOM MUSIC CO.
All Rights Reserved

WHY DON'T YOU BE-LIEVE ME It just is-n't fair

Here, is a heart, that is lone-ly Here, is a heart, you can take

Here, is a heart, for you on-ly, That you can keep or break.

How else can I tell you What more can I do

WHY DON'T YOU BE-LIEVE ME I love on-ly you. you.

Be Sure to Pick Up Three More Great Highlights Song Books

Each Completely Different — Each With Complete Piano/Vocal Arrangements
Each 192 Page — Each With Many Rare Photos $17.95 each

Highlights of the 20's & 30's
Catalog No. 07-1093
Contains:
Ain't Misbehavin'
All Of Me
April In Paris
April Showers
Baby Face
(The) Best Things In Life Are Free
(The) Birth Of The Blues
Breezin' Along With The Breeze
California, Here I Come
(The) Continental
Darn That Dream
Do It Again
Dream A Little Dream Of Me
Find Out What They Like
Guilty
Honeysuckle Rose
I Can't Give You Anything But Love
I Cried For You
I Don't Know Why
I Found A Million Dollar Baby
I Like The Likes Of You
I Thought About You
If You Knew Susie
I'll Build A Stairway To Paradise
I'm Gonna Sit Right Down And Write Myself A Letter
Is It True What They Say About Dixie?
It All Depends On You
It Had To Be You
I've Got The World On A String
(The) Joint Is Jumpin'
June Night
Look For The Silver Lining
Margie
(The) One I Love Belongs To Somebody Else
Somebody Loves Me
St. Louis Blues
Stormy Weather
They Didn't Believe Me
Together
Tuxedo Junction
Until The Real Thing Comes Along
What's New?
When I Take My Sugar To Tea
When It's Sleepy Time Down South
When You're Smiling
Who's Sorry Now?
You Better Go Now
You're My Everything

Highlights of the 60's & 70's
Catalog No. 07-1088
Contains:
Baby Don't Go
Beach Baby
Brown Eyed Girl
Can't Take My Eyes Off Of You
Chuck E.'s In Love
Come A Little Bit Closer
Crazy Love
Donna The Prima Donna
Do That To Me One More Time
867-5309/Jenny
Everybody's Talkin'
Feel Like Makin' Love
Garden Party
Goodbye Cruel World
Hang On Sloopy
Here Comes The Sun
(A) House Is Not A Home
Houston
I Can See Clearly Now
I Got Love
I Know
I'd Really Love To See You Tonight
In The Navy
Johnny Angel
Just One Look
Let The Good Times Roll
Lonely Boy
Look In My Eyes
Love Is The Answer
Midnight Confessions
Mountain Of Love
Nice To Be With You
(The) Night Has a Thousand Eyes
One
Please Love Me Forever
Rescue Me
Save It For A Rainy Day
Shame, Shame, Shame
Smoky Places
Something
Sugar Town
Sun Ain't Gonna Shine Anymore
Surfer Girl
Swearin' To God
Tell It Like It Is
These Boots Are Made For Walkin'
Time Is On My Side
Tiny Bubbles
Torn Between Two Lovers
Trapped By A Thing Called Love
Unchain My Heart
(The) Way I Want To Touch You
We're All Alone
Without You

Highlights of the 70's & 80's
Catalog No. 07-1089
Contains:
Ain't No Sunshine
Alone Again (Naturally)
Angel In Your Arms
Baby Come Back
Bad Case of Lovin' You
Break It To Me Gently
C'est La Vie
China Girl
Cool Night
Coward Of The County
Fire And Ice
Fooled Around And Fell In Love
Handy Man
Hot Rod Hearts
I Believe In You
I'd Like To Teach The World To Sing
I Love Rock 'N Roll
Just When I Needed You Most
La Bamba
Love Hurts
Lovin' You
Mandy
Miami, My Amy
My Sweet Lord
(There's) No Gettin' Over Me
Ocean Front Property
Old Flame
On and On
Queen of Hearts
Sharing The Night Together
She's A Bad Mama Jama
Steal Away
Sunshine (Go Away Today)
Superstar
(The) Sweetest Thing (I've Ever Known)
Third-Rate Romance
This Masquerade
Tonight
Tuff Enuff
Walking On A Thin Line
We're In This Love Together
What A Fool Believes
What I Did For Love
Wildflower
Will The Wolf Survive?
Y.M.C.A.

ALL OF THE ABOVE BOOKS AVAILABLE AT MUSIC STORES EVERYWHERE!
If unable to locate send $17.95 each plus $2.00 per order for shipping to:
CREATIVE CONCEPTS, 410 Bryant Circle, Box 848, Ojai, California 93024